Blender Compositing and Post Processing

Learn the techniques required to create believable and stunning visuals with Blender Compositor

Mythravarun Vepakomma

BIRMINGHAM - MUMBAI

Blender Compositing and Post Processing

First published: January 2014

Production Reference: 1140114

Published by Packt Publishing Ltd.

Livery Place
35 Livery Street
Birmingham B3 2PB, UK.

ISBN 978-1-78216-112-7

www.packtpub.com

Cover Image by Mythravarun Vepakomma (mythravarun@gmail.com)

Credits

Author
Mythravarun Vepakomma

Reviewers
Olivier Amrein
Alexey Dorokhov

Acquisition Editor
Neha Nagwekar

Lead Technical Editor
Mohammed Fahad

Technical Editors
Pramod Kumavat
Adrian Raposo
Gaurav Thingalaya

Copy Editors
Aditya Nair
Stuti Srivastava

Project Coordinator
Michelle Quadros

Proofreader
Ameesha Green

Indexers
Hemangini Bari
Mariammal Chettiyar
Tejal R. Soni

Production Coordinator
Komal Ramchandani

Cover Work
Komal Ramchandani

About the Author

Mythravarun Vepakomma was born in Hyderabad, India, in 1983 and is currently working as a CG Supervisor at Xentrix Studios Pvt Ltd, India. Though he graduated in Electrical and Electronics Engineering in 2004, he has always had a great passion for comics and cartoons. During his studies, his passion got him attracted to web designing and 3D animation.

Mythravarun always believed in transforming his passion into a career. He decided to go for it and started learning 3D graphics and web designing on his own. He also started working as a part-time illustrator and graphic designer. After consistent efforts, he finally moved into the field of 3D animation in 2005 to chase his dream of making it his career.

He has a decade of experience in several TV series, theme park ride films, and features. He now deals with creating and setting up CG lighting and compositing pipelines, providing a creative direction for CG Projects, research and development on several render engines to create a stable future for the studio, and many more things.

Midway through his career, Mythravarun encountered Blender and was fascinated by its features and the fact that it was an open source software. This made him dig deeper into Blender to get a better understanding. Now he prefers to use Blender for many of his illustrations.

As a hobby and secondary interest, he composes music and writes blogs on social awareness. His online presence can be found at the following links:

Personal website: www.mythravarun.com

Blog: www.senseandessence.com

Music and entertainment: www.charliesmile.com

www.youtube.com/thevroad

www.youtube.com/joyasysnthesis

http://joyasynthesis.blogspot.in

Acknowledgments

I thank my wife, Harini Vepakomma, in facilitating and supporting me in writing this wonderful book. I appreciate my loving son, Sri Vishnu Sushane Vepakomma, who allowed me to concentrate on writing the book instead of spending time with him. I also thank the Packt Publishing team for providing me with this opportunity and their support. I am grateful to everyone in my career who helped me gain knowledge and build my personality.

About the Reviewers

Olivier Amrein is a generalist in 3D art and is based in Switzerland. He worked and has given presentations in the following countries: Switzerland, China, Netherlands, Venezuela, Brazil, and Russia.

> I would like to acknowledge and thank my wife and my two lovely kids, Milla and Louis.

Alexey Dorokhov is a software developer. His professional interests include distributed systems, network protocols, and machine learning. Alexey enjoys experimenting with real-time 3D graphics. He prepares most of his 3D assets in Blender, which involves some low poly modeling and lots of scripting.

www.PacktPub.com

Support files, eBooks, discount offers and more

You might want to visit www.PacktPub.com for support files and downloads related to your book.

Did you know that Packt offers eBook versions of every book published, with PDF and ePub files available? You can upgrade to the eBook version at www.PacktPub.com and as a print book customer, you are entitled to a discount on the eBook copy. Get in touch with us at service@packtpub.com for more details.

At www.PacktPub.com, you can also read a collection of free technical articles, sign up for a range of free newsletters and receive exclusive discounts and offers on Packt books and eBooks.

http://PacktLib.PacktPub.com

Do you need instant solutions to your IT questions? PacktLib is Packt's online digital book library. Here, you can access, read and search across Packt's entire library of books.

Why Subscribe?

- Fully searchable across every book published by Packt
- Copy and paste, print and bookmark content
- On demand and accessible via web browser

Free Access for Packt account holders

If you have an account with Packt at www.PacktPub.com, you can use this to access PacktLib today and view nine entirely free books. Simply use your login credentials for immediate access.

With lots of love and respect, I dedicate this book to my dad, Madhusudana Rao Vepakomma and to my mom, Vasantha Lakshmi Vepakomma.

Table of Contents

Preface

Blender Compositing and Post Processing is a one-stop solution to attain state-of-the-art compositing skills to create mind-blowing visuals and productive composites using Blender Compositor.

What this book covers

Chapter 1, Blender Compositing – Overview, provides a basic understanding of the role of compositing in a CG workflow and Blender's importance as a compositor. It also provides an understanding of what can go in and out of Blender Compositor in terms of formats, color space, passes, layers, and bit depths.

Chapter 2, Working with Blender Compositor, explains the Blender Compositor's node-based architecture, different types of nodes, and working in linear workspace using color management. Many useful compositor shortcut keys are detailed in this chapter.

Chapter 3, Working with Input and Output Nodes, covers different ways to get data in and out of Blender Compositor. These nodes essentially form the head and tail of the compositing flow.

Chapter 4, Image Manipulation Techniques, explains the different image manipulation nodes and their utilization procedures available in Blender Compositor. These nodes play a major role in grading a footage to attain a desired look.

Chapter 5, Beyond Grading, deals with advanced compositing techniques beyond grading. These techniques emphasize alternate methods in Blender Compositing for some specific 3D render requirements that can save lots of render times, thereby also saving budgets in making a CG film.

Chapter 6, Alpha Sports, provides an understanding of the significance of the alpha channel and some issues related to it. Different matte extraction techniques such as keying, Matte ID, and masking are detailed in this chapter through practical examples.

What you need for this book

Readers should have basic lighting and shading knowledge of Blender to be able to comprehend and extract the required passes for compositing. Blender 2.68 is used in this book.

Who this book is for

This book is for digital CG artists longing to add photo realism and life to their footage. This book also assists technical CG artists to strategize and implement productive lighting and compositing pipeline in CG filmmaking. If you are new to Blender or compositing, do not worry because this book guides you using a step-by-step approach to help you gain compositing skills.

Conventions

In this book, you will find a number of styles of text that distinguish between different kinds of information. Here are some examples of these styles and an explanation of their meaning.

New terms and **important words** are shown in bold. Words that you see on the screen, in menus or dialog boxes for example, appear in the text like this:"**Relighting** is a compositing technique to add extra light information."

Tips and tricks are shown like this.

Reader feedback

Feedback from our readers is always welcome. Let us know what you think about this book—what you liked or may have disliked. Reader feedback is important for us to develop titles that you really get the most out of.

To send us general feedback, simply send an e-mail to feedback@packtpub.com, and mention the book title through the subject of your message.

If there is a topic that you have expertise in and you are interested in either writing or contributing to a book, see our author guide on www.packtpub.com/authors.

Customer support

Now that you are the proud owner of a Packt book, we have a number of things to help you to get the most from your purchase.

Downloading the color images of this book

We also provide you a PDF file that has color images of the screenshots/diagrams used in this book. The color images will help you better understand the changes in the output. You can download this file from: http://www.packtpub.com/sites default/files/downloads/1127os_graphics.pdf.

Errata

Although we have taken every care to ensure the accuracy of our content, mistakes do happen. If you find a mistake in one of our books—maybe a mistake in the text or the code—we would be grateful if you would report this to us. By doing so, you can save other readers from frustration and help us improve subsequent versions of this book. If you find any errata, please report them by visiting http://www.packtpub.com/support, selecting your book, clicking on the **errata submission form** link, and entering the details of your errata. Once your errata are verified, your submission will be accepted and the errata will be uploaded to our website, or added to any list of existing errata, under the Errata section of that title.

Piracy

Piracy of copyright material on the Internet is an ongoing problem across all media. At Packt, we take the protection of our copyright and licenses very seriously. If you come across any illegal copies of our works, in any form, on the Internet, please provide us with the location address or website name immediately so that we can pursue a remedy.

Please contact us at copyright@packtpub.com with a link to the suspected pirated material.

We appreciate your help in protecting our authors, and our ability to bring you valuable content.

Questions

You can contact us at questions@packtpub.com if you are having a problem with any aspect of the book, and we will do our best to address it.

1

Blender Compositing – Overview

This chapter provides a basic understanding on the role of compositing in a CG workflow and Blender's importance as a compositor. The following is a list of topics covered in this chapter:

- Compositing significance in the CG pipeline
- Significance of Blender as a compositor
- Blender-supported formats
- Blender color modes and depths
- Blender color spaces
- Understanding the render layers and render passes concepts

Understanding CG compositing

CG compositing is an assembly of multiple images that are merged and modified to make a final image. Compositing happens after 3D rendering, as seen in a typical CG pipeline flow, which is the most expensive phase of CG filmmaking. A well planned lighting and compositing pipeline can optimize render resources and also provide unlimited image manipulation functionalities to achieve the desired look for the film. Though compositing is at the end of the pipeline, with its wide range of toolsets, it can help to avoid the work of going back to previous departments in the CG pipeline.

The following diagram depicts a CG pipeline flow and also shows where the composite process fits in:

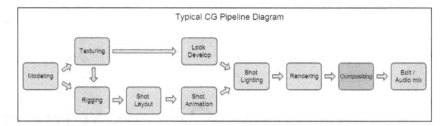

The strength of compositing lies in modifying the rendered CG footage into a believable output. The following screenshot portrays a **Composited Output** image done from rendered passes. Many effects such as glare, color corrections, and defocus make the output seem more believable than the rendered beauty pass, which is shown as the first image in **Render Passes**.

Compositing also provides tools to grade an image to achieve extreme or fantasy style outputs. The following screenshot illustrates different types of grades that can be performed:

Blender's significance as a compositor

Blender is the only open source product with a range of features comparable to other industry standard commercial or proprietary software. It provides a unique advantage of combining 3D and 2D stages of CG filmmaking into one complete package. This gives tremendous control when planning and executing a CG pipeline. Automating and organizing data flow from 3D rendering to compositing can be achieved more easily in Blender compared to other solutions, since compositing software is separate from the 3D rendering software.

Getting started

To be able to get most out of Blender Compositor, it is essential to have a superficial understanding of what Blender can offer. This includes supporting formats, color modes, color spaces, render layers, and render passes.

Supported image formats in Blender

Blender's image input/output system supports regular 32 bit graphics (4 x 8 bits) or floating point images that store 128 bits per pixel (4 x 32 bits) or 64 bits per pixel (4 x 16 bits). This includes texture mapping, background images, and the compositor. These attributes are available in output properties as shown in following screenshot:

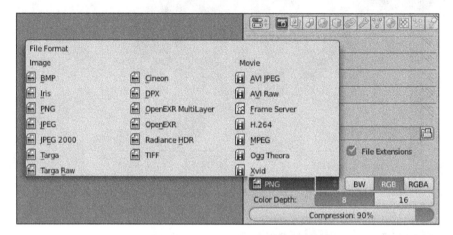

Supported color modes in Blender

The color modes are the options available to view the channel information of a footage, they are:

- **BW**: Images get saved in 8 bits grayscale (only PNG, JPEG, TGA, and TIF)
- **RGB**: Images are saved with RGB (color)
- **RGBA**: Images are saved with RGB and Alpha data (if supported)

Supported color depths in Blender

Image color depth, also called bit depth, is the number of bits used for each color component of a single pixel. Blender supports 8, 10, 12, 16, and 32 bit color channels.

Blender's color spaces

The mathematical representation of a set of colors is termed as color space. Each color space has a specific significance and provides unique ways to perform image manipulation. Depending on the task in hand, the color space can be chosen. Blender supports the RGB color space, the HSV color space, the YUV color space, and the YCbCr color space.

The RGB color space

The RGB (red, green, and blue) color space is widely used in computer graphics due to the fact that color displays use red, green, and blue as three primary additive colors to create the desired color. This choice simplifies the system's design and you can benefit from a large number of existing software routines since this color space has been around for a number of years. However, RGB is not suitable when working with real-world images. All three RGB components should be of equal bandwidth to generate a color, resulting in a frame buffer that has the same pixel depth and display resolution for each RGB component. So, irrespective of modifying the image for luminance or color, all three channels have to be read, processed, and stored. To avoid these limitations, many video standards use color spaces that provide luma and color as separate signals.

The HSV color space

HSV stands for hue, saturation, and value. This color space provides flexibility to be able to modify hue, saturation, and value independently. HSV is a cylindrical co-ordinate representation of points in an RGB color model. The following screenshot shows RGB in comparison to HSV values to attain a red color:

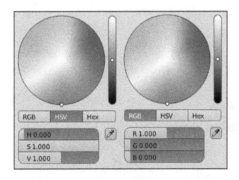

The YUV color space

The YUV color space is used by the **Phase Alternating Line (PAL)**, **National Television System Committee (NTSC)**, and **Sequential Color with Memory (SECAM)** composite color video standards for color televisions. Y stands for the luma component (the brightness), and U and V are the chrominance (color) components. This color space was intended to provide luma information for black and white television systems and color information for color television systems. Now, YUV is a color space typically used as part of a color image or CG pipeline to enable developers and artists to work separately with luminance and color information of an image.

The YCbCr color space

The YCbCr color space was developed as a digital component video standard, which is a scaled and offset version of the YUV color space. Y is the luma component and Cb and Cr are the blue-difference and red-difference chroma components. While YUV is used for analog color encoding in television systems, YCbCr is used for digital color encoding suitable for video and still-image compressions and transmissions, such as MPEG and JPEG.

Render layers/passes

To optimize render resources and also be able to provide full control at the compositing stage, a CG lighting scene is split into multiple render layers and render passes.

Render layers

A typical lighting scene consists of two to three characters, props, and one set. To provide an opportunity to re-render only required elements in the scene, each element is separated into its own render layer for rendering. All interaction renders are also separated into render layers. The following list shows a typical render layer classification.

- Character 1
- Character 2
- Character 3
- Characters cast shadow
- Characters occlusion
- Set
- Set occlusion
- Set interaction with characters

Render passes

Passes or AOVs (arbitrary output variables) are intermediate computational results that are shown when rendering a layer. All render passes are buffered out when rendering a render layer and written as separate data. These passes can be utilized in compositing to rebuild the beauty of the render layer and also allow us to tweak individual shader/light contributions. The following screenshot shows the Blender internal render engine's **Passes** panel:

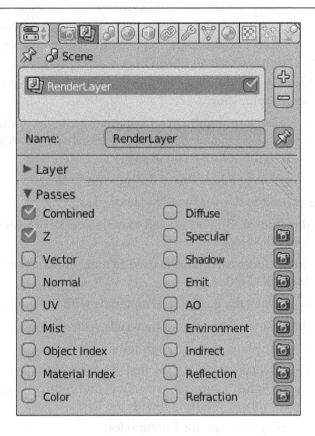

Every render layer in Blender, by default, is equipped with these render passes, but the content in the render passes is based on the data available to the render layer. However, the pass definition and the type of content it stores doesn't vary. All passes that have a camera icon beside them can be excluded from the combined pass data by clicking on the camera icon. This provides another level of control over the content of the combined pass.

Each passes' significance and content

The following screenshot shows outputs of different render passes available, by default, in Blender's internal render engine. Their significance is explained as follows:

- **Combined**: This renders everything in the image, even if it's not necessary. This includes all the options blended into a single output, except those options that you've indicated should be omitted from this pass as indicated with the camera button.

- **Z (Z depth)**: This map shows how far away each pixel is from the camera. It is used for **depth of field (DOF)**. The depth map is inverse linear (1/distance) from the camera position.

- **Vector**: This indicates the direction and speed of things that are moving. It is used with Vector Blur.

- **Normal**: This calculates lighting and apparent geometry for a bump map (an image that is used to fake details of an object) or to change the apparent direction of the light falling on an object.

- **UV**: This allows us to add textures during compositing.

- **Mist**: This is used to deliver the Mist factor pass.

- **Object Index** (IndexOB): This is used to make masks of selected objects using the Matte ID Node.

- **Material Index** (IndexMA): This is used to make masks of selected material using the Matte ID Node.

- **Color**: This displays the flat color of materials without shading information.

- **Diffuse**: This displays the color of materials with shading information.

- **Specular**: This displays specular highlights.

- **Shadow**: This displays the shadows that can be cast. Make sure shadows are cast by your lights (positive or negative) and received by materials. To use this pass, mix or multiply it with the **Diffuse** pass.

- **Emit**: This displays the options for emission pass.

- **AO**: This displays ambient occlusion.

- **Environment**: This displays the environment lighting contribution.

- **Indirect**: This displays the indirect lighting contribution.

- **Reflection**: This displays the reflection contributions based on shader attributes that are, participating in the current render.

- **Refraction**: This displays the refraction contributions based on shader attributes that are participating in the current render.

The following screenshot shows some outputs of Blender's default render passes:

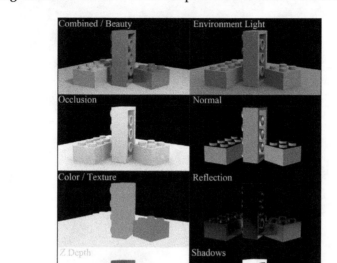

Summary

This chapter introduced the CG compositing stage and Blender's significant advantage as a compositor. We also obtained an understanding on what can go in and out of Blender Compositor in terms of formats, color spaces, passes, layers, and bit depths. The next chapter deals with Blender's node-based architecture and user interface.

Working with Blender Compositor

2

This chapter explains the node-based architecture of Blender Compositor, linear workflow, and user interface panels. Following is the list of topics covered in this chapter:

- Node-based architecture
- Types of compositing nodes
- Node Editor
- UV / Image Editor
- Color management and linear workspace

Architecture

Blender Compositor is built on an efficient **node-based** architecture. Every transformation tool in Blender Compositor is defined as a **node**, building a **directed acyclic graph (DAG)** from source input to output image. This process of building graphs using individual transformation tools is termed as node-based workflow. This architecture provides flexibility to tweak parameters procedurally. The connectors that connect these individual nodes are called **noodles**.

Composite node types

Every individual node performs a specific operation, and many such nodes are linked progressively to form a compositing flow. These nodes can be classified into three categories based on the functional similarities:

- **Input nodes**: These nodes are used to get the image's information into Blender Compositor's workspace
- **Output nodes**: These nodes save or display the result of the node graph
- **Transformation nodes**: These nodes are used to modify or combine the input media

Getting familiar with the compositing user interface

Blender Compositor UI is very intuitive yet powerful. Layout switcher, shown in following screenshot, can be used to switch to the compositing workspace. This UI primarily consists of two modules:

- **Node Editor**: This is the workspace where the node graph can be built
- **UV Image Editor**: This is to view the result of a complete node graph or part of it

Alternatively, the UI can be customized by splitting or joining the layout as per requirement, as shown in the following screenshot. Moving the pointer to any edge of the panel turns the pointer into a two-sided arrow. Then, right-clicking will show you options to split or merge the panel as per your requirement. The customized layout can be saved as a scene preset in layout switcher.

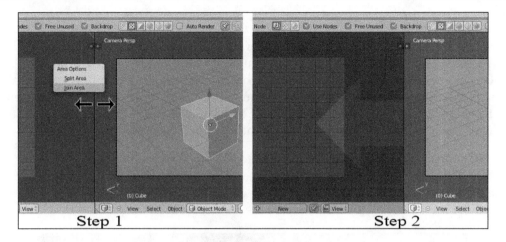

The following screenshot shows a typical compositing environment with all the relevant panels:

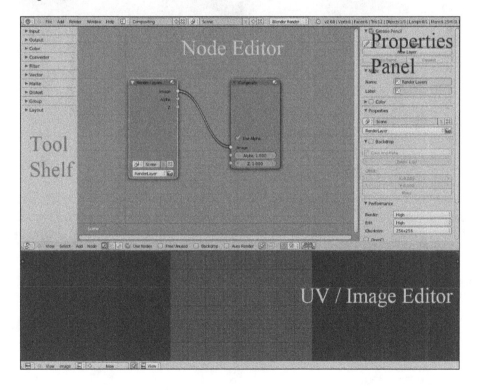

Node Editor

The **Node Editor** has a menu panel and workspace area as shown in following screenshot. The menu panel has all the menu items required to create the nodes and view options. The workspace area is where the graph will be built. As an initial set up, the **Use Nodes** checkbox in the menu panel has to be checked. The **Add** menu in the menu panel can be used to find all of the available Blender' Compositor nodes, which will automatically be populated in the workspace area when selected.

The **Backdrop** checkbox provides a means to be able to project the viewer node's output as background in the workspace area. When working in the Node Editor, use the left mouse button to move the selected nodes, roll the mouse roller to zoom the view, click on the node, and move the mouse roller to pan the view:

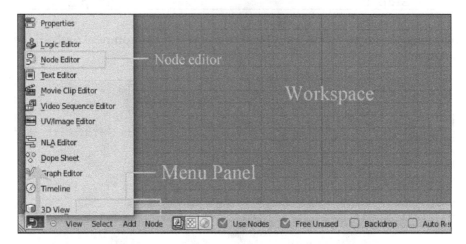

Media can be dragged and dropped on to the Node Editor's workspace. All nodes can be connected using the round dots called **sockets** attached to nodes. To be able to view the image in backdrop, we need to check **Use Nodes** and create a viewer node by navigating to **Add | Output | Viewer**, as shown in the following screenshot. Then, the connections can be made by clicking and dragging on the round socket dots and dropping them on the input socket dot of the other node.

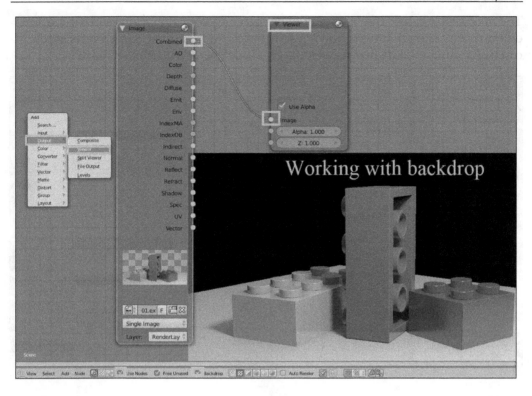

When **Use Nodes** is enabled, Blender creates a render layer and composite nodes by default. The render layer carries the 3D render data from the current Blender scene file. **Composite** node renders the result of the node flow connected to it when the render is invoked (the *F12* key for current frame or *Ctrl + F12* for animation). This is done by switching on the **Compositing** checkbox in the **Post Processing** option in the properties editor, as shown in following screenshot:

The noodles curvature can be modified by selecting **User Preferences** in the current editor type as shown in the following screenshot. Alternatively, **User Preferences** can be found in the **File** menu available on top-left screen of the Blender UI:

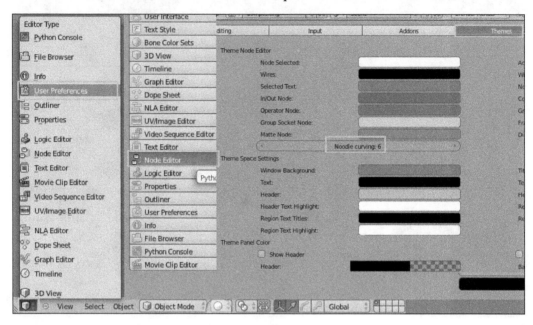

UV / Image Editor

UV Image Editor also has a menu panel and workspace area. As shown in the following screenshot, **Browser** helps in choosing which output to be viewed and **Pass Select** helps in showing the render passes of the media selected in the browser. This selected data is displayed in the workspace area. An advantage of using this editor to view the output instead of the backdrop in the Node Editor is that the left mouse click shows pixel information, such as R, G, B, H, S, V, and A:

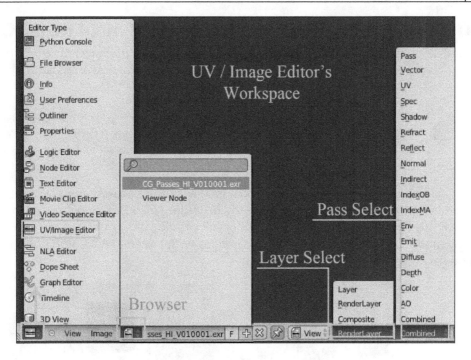

UV / Image Editor also provides histogram and waveform displays, shown in the following screenshot, to perform precise grading. These options can be displayed by clicking on the **Scopes** menu item in the **View** menu as shown in following screenshot:

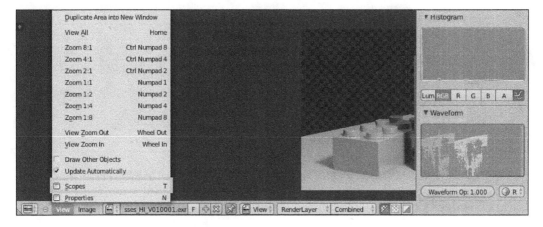

Color management and linear workspace

Display devices don't display the images exactly as they get them but rather display them with reduced gamma values, as represented in the following screenshot.

 Gamma is a unit that describes the relationship between the voltage input and the brightness of the image on your display screen. It defines the relation between the numerical value of a pixel and its actual luminance.

All digital image-processing software saves images with increased gamma values to counter the loss in display, thereby providing an accurate picture to the user. All this happens behind the UI and doesn't provide any control to the user. So, any modifications attempted on these images with baked gamma will not provide expected results.

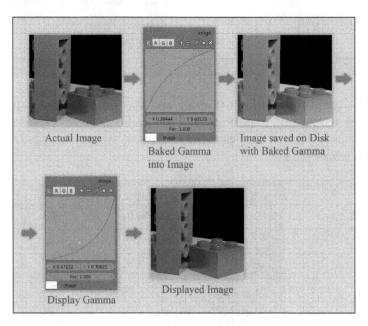

Color management will help in creating a workflow that allows the user to work on the actual image instead of the gamma-corrected image. The following screenshot shows Blender's **Color Management** options:

When color management is enabled, it introduces a reverse gamma curve on the image to switch it back to original gamma and also applies gamma correction before sending it to the display device. This work state is termed as **linear workspace**, explained in following screenshot:

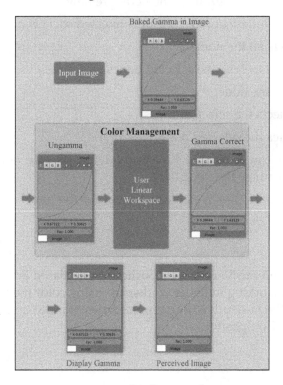

Handy shortcuts for Blender Compositor

Blender, by default, is equipped with shortcuts for most of the commonly used operations. The following list highlights shortcuts that will come in handy when working in Compositor:

- *Shift + A*: This displays the **Add** menu at the pointer's location.
- *Ctrl + Shift +* left mouse button: Applying this on any node connects its first output socket to the viewer node. Repeating this multiple times will cycle the connections on all the available output sockets.
- *Ctrl +* left mouse button: This is used to cut the noodle connections.
- *X*: This deletes the selected node.
- *Ctrl + X*: This deletes the current node and connects the previous node to the next node.
- *Alt +* middle mouse button: This pans the backdrop image.
- *Shift + D*: This duplicates the selected node or noodle network.
- *Ctrl +* left mouse button: This toggles between layout presets.
- *H*: This collapses the node.
- *Shift + H*: This hides/unhides the node preview.
- *Ctrl + H*: This hides/unhides the unconnected sockets of a selected node.
- *A*: This selects all the nodes.
- *B*: This is used to drag the selected nodes.
- *G*: This grabs the node.
- *F*: This connects the selected nodes.
- *M*: This mutes the selected node.
- *S* or *R*: These can be used to scale or rotate the selected nodes. This is useful to rearrange the node flow.
- *Shift +* Space bar: This maximizes/minimizes the panel.

Summary

This chapter explained the Blender Compositor's node-based architecture, different types of nodes, and working in linear workspace using color management. The next chapter deals with the in-depth working procedures of input and output nodes available in Blender Compositor.

3
Working with Input and Output Nodes

This chapter illustrates all the input and output nodes available in Blender Compositor, essential for importing or exporting data from it. The following is the list of topics covered in this chapter:

- Input nodes
- Output nodes

How to import or export from a compositor?

Input nodes are used to import footage into the Node Editor. Output nodes are used to export or display the result of a node graph. So, these nodes form the head and tail of the node flow drawn in Blender's node graph UI.

Input nodes

Input nodes are used to generate footage or to feed footage into the flow. These nodes don't have any input sockets. At any instance, there will be multiple types of inputs that a node flow might require, as shown in following screenshot and listed as follows:

- A color or value
- A procedurally generated pattern or texture
- A rendered static or sequence of images

- A movie clip
- Data rendered through the active camera of the current scene

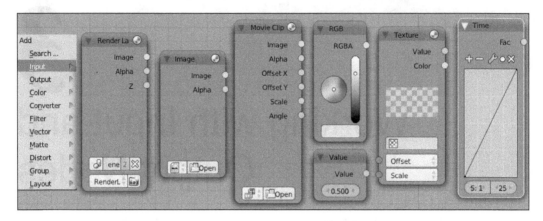

The Render Layers node

The **Render Layers** node inputs the rendered data through the active camera of the current scene. As shown in following screenshot, the node displays all the available passes, render layers and scenes present in the current rendered file. Multiple **Render Layers** nodes can be used to pick different layers or scenes from the rendered data of the current Blender file:

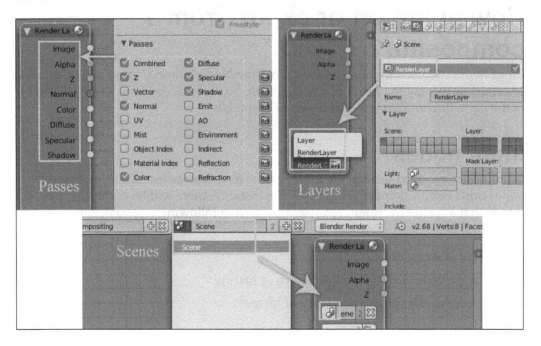

The Image node

The **Image** node loads images or image sequences into the Node Editor, exposing all channels of the image. This node can also input the **Alpha** and **Z** depth channels, if the image contains them. An image that's loaded in the UV Image Editor can also be picked using this node. Dragging and dropping an image into the Node Editor automatically loads the image into the **Image** node. When **OpenEXR Multilayer** is chosen as the format for a render image in render settings, all enabled render passes are stored in the same image. After rendering, this image can be dragged on to the Node Editor; Blender imports the image using the Image node, with all passes saved in their respective buffers.

The Movie Clip node

The **Movie Clip** node can load any movie file supported by Blender. The open folder icon is used to browse the required clip.

The RGB node

The **RGB** node loads a fixed color. The color can be chosen from the color wheel and a vertical value bar seen on the node. Alternatively, a bigger color wheel can be obtained by clicking on the colored rectangle at the bottom of the node. This value can be inserted to animate the image by right-clicking on it and clicking on **Insert Keyframe**.

The Value node

Similar to the RGB node, the **Value** node loads a constant value to the flow. The Value slider provided at the bottom of the node can be used to attain the required value. A value can be manually entered by left-clicking the slider or by left-clicking on it, holding, and dragging the values. This value can be keyed to animate by right-clicking on it and clicking on **Insert Keyframe**.

The Texture node

The **Texture** node can load any texture that's available in the current Blender file or from Blender's procedural texture library, as shown in following screenshot:

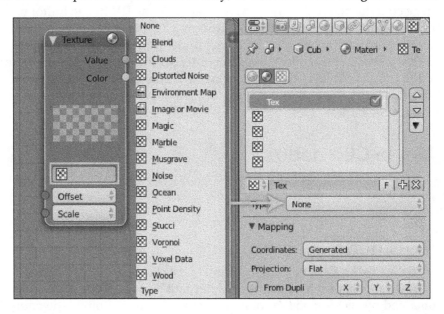

The **Color** socket outputs the RGB channel of the texture and the **Value** socket outputs the Luminance channel of the texture. The **Offset** and **Scale** parameters can be used to modify the texture. This modification will not affect the texture itself.

The Time node

The **Time** node also loads a value similar to a value node, but the difference is that this value can be altered over time using the curve. The start and end frames will signify the frames in which the curve affects the flow.

The Mask node

The **Mask** node can be used to create shape masks by picking mask's data blocks in the browse ID data block. These mask's data blocks can be created in the UV Image Editor by choosing the **Mask** mode as the editing context, shown in following screenshot. These masks, generated using the **Mask** node, can be used in the compositing flow to modify the pixels inside or outside the mask shape.

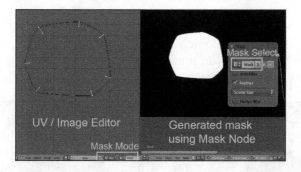

The Bokeh Image node

The **Bokeh Image** node can be used to create a custom bokeh shape. This shape can be connected to the **Bokeh Blur** node, which then uses this shape as the bokeh shape, as shown in following screenshot:

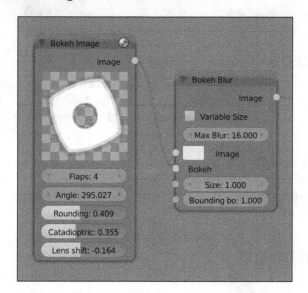

The description of the node is as follows:

- **Flaps** control the number of sides of the bokeh shape
- **Angle** rotates the bokeh shape
- **Rounding** reduces the sharpness at the corners of the sides
- **Catadioptric** creates and increases empty pixels from inside the bokeh shape
- **Lens Shift** adds a chromatic aberration effect to the shape, splitting the shape with color offsets

Output nodes

Output nodes should be used to fetch data from the compositor and to view it in the UV / Image Editor or save it as an image or image sequence. Different output nodes are shown in following screenshot:

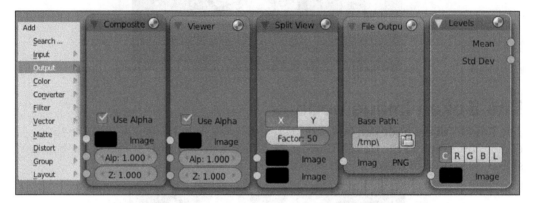

The Composite node

The **Composite** node connects the output of a composite flow to the renderer. Connecting a node to the **Composite** node will output the result till the connected node, when rendered. Leaving the **Composite** node unconnected will output a blank image. Having multiple composite nodes might give unpredictable results.

The **Image**, **Alpha**, and **Z** input sockets store the corresponding connected results into the respective image channels. The **Z** input can be used only if the EXR format is chosen as the output format. This node can also be used to route the output to the UV / Image Editor.

The Viewer node

The **Viewer** node is a handy tool to inspect the compositing flow. Using this node, the output can be tunneled to backdrop of the Node Editor or the UV / Image Editor.

The Split Viewer node

The **Split Viewer** node allows you to inspect two images or two parts of the compositing flow. Clicking on **X** will display a side-by-side comparison and clicking on **Y** will display a top-down comparison. The image connected to the top socket is displayed either on the right or on top of the window. The slider provides an adjustment to the location of the split between the two sockets in the viewer.

The File Output node

The **File Output** node can simulate **AOVs (arbitrary output values)** from the compositing flow, similar to rendering passes from a render layer. Connecting this node to any other node will write an image from the calculations done till the connected node.

The Levels node

Connecting the **Levels** node to an image can output the value of a selected component of the image. Combined RGB, Red, Green, Blue, or Luminance channels can be read from the connected image. It can output mean/average values or a standard deviation, which measures the diversity of values.

Summary

This chapter covered different ways to get data in and out of Blender Compositor. This essentially forms the head and tail of the compositing flow.

The next chapter will demonstrate image manipulation techniques using various Blender Compositor nodes.

4
Image Manipulation Techniques

This chapter explains the different image manipulation nodes and their utilization procedures that are available in Blender Compositor. These nodes play a major role in attaining the desired look. The following is a list of topics covered in this chapter:

- The Bright/Contrast node
- The Hue Saturation Value node
- The Color Correction node
- Significance of Gain, Gamma, and Lift
- Significance of Midtones, Highlights, and Shadows
- The RGB Curves node
- The Color Balance node
- The Mix node
- The Gamma node
- The Invert node
- The Hue Correct node
- Transformation nodes

Understanding image manipulation

Image manipulation is the main phase for establishing a predetermined look in compositing. This stage mostly involves grading, merging, transforming, and resizing of the footage to achieve the desired look of the film. Blender Compositor is equipped with various tool nodes to perform these tasks.

The Bright/Contrast node

The brightness of an image signifies the amount of light that is reflecting or radiating from it. Increasing or decreasing the brightness of a node proportionally changes the light reflection intensities of the input image as shown in following screenshot:

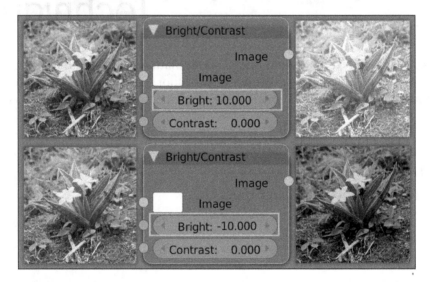

The contrast of an image signifies the luminance and/or color variation; in other words, the separation between the darkest and brightest areas of the image. Increasing the contrast emphasizes the distance between the dark and bright pixels in the image, thus making shadows darker and highlights brighter. This effect makes parts of the image pop up, making it a vibrant image. Decreasing the contrast makes the shadows lighter and highlights darker, making the image dull and less interesting. The following screenshot shows the effect of increasing and decreasing the contrast value on the **Bright/Contrast** node:

The Hue Saturation Value node

The **Hue Saturation Value** node provides a visual spectrum-based image control. The input image can be modified using the hue shift, which ranges from red to violet.

Hue

Using the **Hue** slider, the image hue can be shifted in the visible spectrum range. At the default value of 0.5, the hue doesn't affect the image. Reducing the value from 0.5 to 0 adds more cyan to the image, and increasing the value from 0.5 to 1 adds more reds and greens.

Saturation

Saturation alters the strength of a hue tone in the image. A value of 0 removes the hue tones, making the image greyscale. A value of 2 doubles the strength of the hue tones.

Value

Modifying **Value** affects the luminance of the color in the image. Increasing **Value** makes an image lighter, and decreasing **Value** makes the image darker.

Factor

Factor (**Fac**) determines how much this node affects the image. A factor of 0 means that the input image is not affected by this node.

The following screenshot shows how **Hue**, **Saturation**, and **Value** will affect the input image:

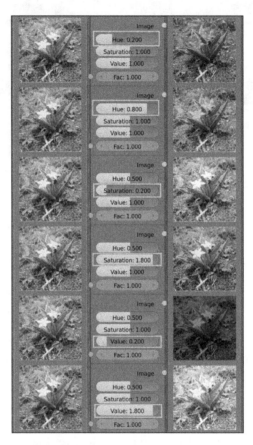

The Color Correction node

The **Color Correction** node provides three dimensional controls on the input image as shown in following screenshot. As the first dimension, all vertical columns provide control on **Saturation**, **Contrast**, **Gamma**, **Gain**, and **Lift**. As the second dimension, all horizontal rows provide control on **Master**, **Highlights**, **Midtones**, and **Shadows**. The third dimensional control is **Red**, **Green**, and **Blue**. This node provides numerous combinations to arrive at a desired result through the use of these three dimensional controls.

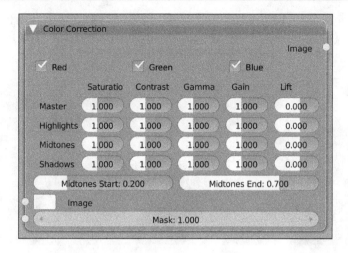

Master, Highlights, Midtones, and Shadows

The tonal information of the image can be divided into **Shadows**, **Midtones**, and **Highlights**. As shown in the following screenshot, this information can be represented as a histogram. In this representation, the left-hand values relate to the dark tones (**Shadows**), the middle values relate to **Midtones**, and the right-hand values relate to **Highlights**.

The **Midtones Start** and **Midtones End** sliders of the **Color Correction** node provide flexibility to alter the range between **Shadows**, **Midtones**, and **Highlights** using the luminance of the input image. These sliders don't consider the **Red**, **Green**, and **Blue** checkboxes. Controlling the tonal information through the **Master** attributes influences the complete range in the histogram curve of the image, thereby affecting the whole image.

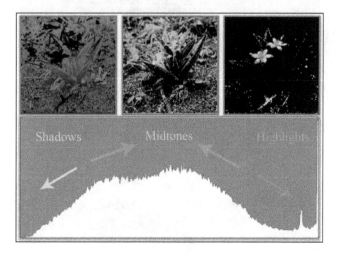

This level of control can be extended to individual red (**R**), green (**G**), blue (**B**), and luminance (**L**) channels of the image to gain more precision. The following screenshot displays histograms of the individual channels:

Gamma, Gain, and Lift

To arrive at a desired result quicker when using a Color Correction node, understanding the difference in control between Gamma, Gain, and Lift is vital. These terms can be understood better using an input (x axis) versus output (y axis) plot, as seen in following screenshot:

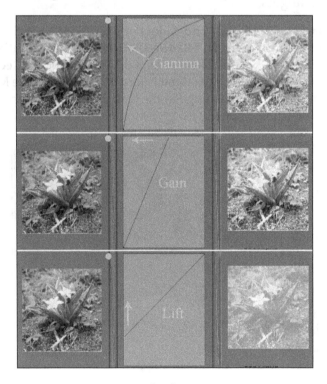

Each of these three properties controls the specific tonal information of an image, summarized as follows:

- **Gamma**: This property controls the curve exponent, affecting the midtones of an image

- **Gain**: This property controls the curve slope, mostly influencing the image highlights

- **Lift**: This property controls the curve offset, mostly influencing the image shadows

Mask socket

The **Mask** socket, also available for many other nodes, can be used to plug a grayscale map to specify the node influence on the output. Node influence will be 100 percent at value **1**.

The RGB Curves node

The **RGB Curves** node provides a Bezier-curve-based control for image grading. This curve represents an input (x axis) versus output (y axis) plot. Modifying this curve remaps the output range, thereby providing a grading effect. This node also provides controls to set up black and white levels for the input image.

A flat image that has all pixel values in the midtones range can be graded to redistribute the pixel values to occupy the complete range of shadows, midtones, and highlights. This makes the image more vibrant and interesting. An example of this grading is shown in the following screenshot. The waveforms and histograms of both the images show the redistribution of pixel values to occupy the complete range and provide a better graded image.

Grading with this node can be done using Bezier curve or by tweaking the black and white levels. An appropriate technique can be adapted based on the task.

Grading by setting the black and white levels

The variation between the black and white levels of an image signifies its contrast. Using the RGB Curves node to increase an image's contrast, instead of using a Bright/Contrast node, gives the advantage of picking samples from the input image, The darkest and the brightest levels of the input image can be picked as black and white levels respectively, as shown in following screenshot. You can pick a sample using the selector that pops up below the color wheel when either **Black Level** or **White Level** is clicked on.

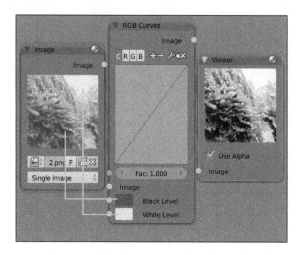

This method not only alters the contrast but also changes hue tones. This change can be nullified by desaturating the black and white levels to zero using the saturation (**S**) slider in the **HSV** mode. The following screenshot shows a change in contrast without hue shifting:

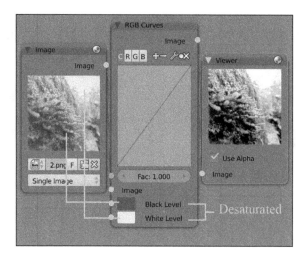

Alternatively, the black and white levels can be adjusted directly using the **HSV** or **RGB** mode in the color wheel that pops up when the small colored rectangular region to the left of **Black Level** or **White Level** is clicked on.

 Grading can be performed on individual red, green, and blue channels by using the **R**, **G**, and **B** switches on the top left of the RGB Curves node. This method provides more precision to achieve better grading.

Grading using the Bezier curve

A similar result, that was achieved in the previous technique, can be achieved by using the Bezier curve. The bottom-left corner (0,0) in the plot is the shadows point. The top-right corner (1,1) in the plot is the highlights point. All points that lie in between these two points signify the midtones. The following screenshot demonstrates grading using the Bezier curve to arrive at a similar result, as achieved using the black and white levels technique:

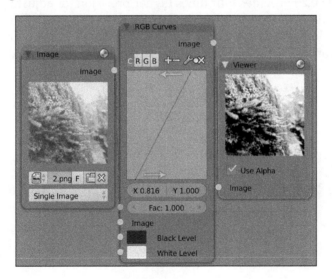

The factor value (**Fac**) in this node represents the influence of this node on the output. An image can be connected to this socket to specify node influence. A value of **1** will display an influence of 100 percent in the output.

The following screenshot specifies a few common grading effects—invert, posterize, lighten, and contrast—performed using the **RGB Curves** node:

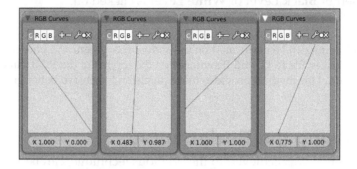

When using the **RGB Curves** node, we will sometimes need higher precision in adjusting the curve points. The default setup makes it tedious to have such precision. This task can be accomplished by having cascaded RGB Curves nodes with different factor values as shown in following screenshot. In the following flow, first grade node with Fac value of **0.25** provides four times higher precision for adjusting shadows, second grade node with **Fac** value of **0.5** provides twice the precision for highlights, and third grade node with Fac value of **1** provides default precision for midtones. A similar flow can be created to have different precisions for **R**, **G**, and **B** channels.

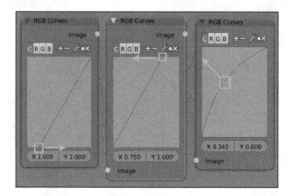

The Color Balance node

The **Color Balance** node provides a control that is similar to the RGB Curves node for grading, as shown in following screenshot. The difference is that since this node has a color wheel for each of the Gain/Gamma/Lift components, its easier to manage color-based grading. The same process in the RGB Curves node would be a bit complicated since curves have to be shaped separately for R, G, and B. However, having a curve-based control in the RGB Curves node provides more precision in grading in comparison to the **Color Balance** node.

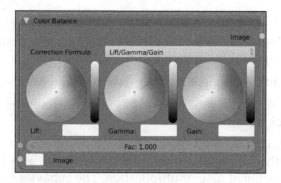

The **Color Balance** and **RGB Curves** nodes can be used in combination to make flows to have the desired grading control.

The Mix node

The **Mix** node blends a base image connected to the top image socket with a second image connected to the bottom image socket based on the selected blending modes, as shown in following screenshot. All individual pixels are mixed based on the mode selected in this node. The Alpha and Z channels are also mixed.

 The output resolution of a Mix node will be the same as the background node resolution.

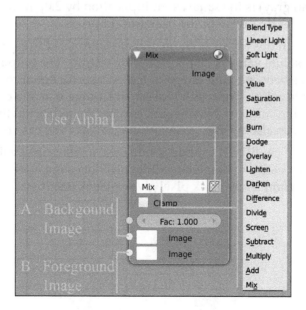

Blending modes

- **Mix**: In this mode, by using the alpha values, the foreground pixels are placed over the background pixels.

- **Add** (A+B): In this mode, the pixels from both images are added.

- **Subtract** (A-B): In this mode, the pixels from the foreground are subtracted from the background.

- **Multiply** (A*B): This mode results in a darker output than either pixel in most cases (the exception is if any of them is white). This works in a similar way to conventional math multiplication. The behavior is opposite to the Screen mode.

- **Screen** [1-(1-A)*(1-B)]: In this mode, both images' pixel values are inverted and multiplied by each other and then the result is again inverted. This outputs a brighter result compared to both input pixels in many cases (except if one of the pixels is black). Black pixels do not change the background pixels at all (and vice versa); similarly, white pixels give a white output. This behavior is the opposite of the **Multiply** mode.

- **Overlay** {If A<=0.5, then (2*A)*B, else 1-[1-2*(A-0.5)]*(1-B)}: This mode is a combination of the **Screen** and **Multiply** modes, and is based on the base color.

- **Divide** (A/B): In this mode, the background pixels are divided by the foreground pixels. If the foreground is white, the background isn't changed. The darker the foreground, the brighter is the output [division by 0.5 (median gray) is the same as multiplication by 2.0]. If the foreground is black, Blender doesn't alter the background pixels.

- **Difference**: In this mode, both images are subtracted from one another and the absolute value is displayed as the output. The output value shows the distance between both images: black stands for equal colors and white for opposite colors. The result looks a bit strange in many cases. This mode can be used to compare two images, and results in black if they are equal. This mode can also be used to invert the pixels of the base image.

- **Darken** [Min (A, B)]: This mode results in a smaller pixel value by comparing both image pixels. A completely white pixel does not affect the background at all and a completely black pixel gives a black result.

- **Lighten** [Max (A, B)]: This mode results in a higher pixel value by comparing both image pixels. A completely black pixel does not alter the image at all and a completely white pixel gives a white result.

- **Dodge** [A/(1-B)]: This mode brightens the image by using the gradient in the other image. It outputs lighter areas of the image where the gradient is whiter.

- **Burn** [1-(1-A)/B]: This mode darkens one socket image on the gradient fed to the other image. It outputs darker images.

- **Color**: In this mode, each pixel is added with its color tint. This can be used to increase the tint of the image.

- **Value**: In this mode, the RGB values from both images are converted to HSV parameters. Both the pixel values are blended, and the hue and saturation of the base image are combined with the blended value and converted to RGB.

- **Saturation**: In this mode, the RGB values of both images are converted to HSV parameters. Both pixels saturations are blended, and the hue and value of the base image are combined with the blended saturation and converted to RGB.

- **Hue**: In this mode, the RGB parameters of both pixels are converted to HSV parameters. Both pixels hues are blended, and the value and saturation of the base image are combined with the blended hue and converted to RGB.

Use Alpha

The **Use Alpha** button of the **Mix** node instructs the **Mix** node to use the Alpha channel available in the foreground image. Based on the grayscale information in the alpha channel, the foreground pixels are made transparent to view the background image. The effect of the selected blending mode is thus seen only in the nontransparent foreground pixels. The Alpha channel of the output image is not affected by this option.

Factor

The factor input field (**Fac**) decides the amount of mixing of the bottom socket. A factor of **0.0** does not use the bottom socket, whereas a value of **1.0** makes full use. In **Mix** mode, 50:50 (**0.50**) is an even mix between the two, but in **Add** mode, **0.50** means that only half of the second socket's influence will be applied.

The following screenshot shows outputs from all the described Mix modes without altering the inputs connected to the top and bottom nodes:

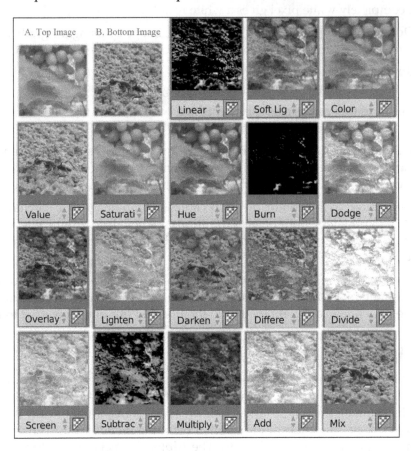

The Gamma node

An overall gamma correction can be made to the final result using the Gamma node. This correction helps to alter the lighting information in the result.

 The gamma value in this node is the gamma correction value. Gamma correction = 1/gamma.

The Invert node

The **Invert** node can invert the pixel values in the RGB or Alpha channel based on what is selected in the node. This node comes in handy during masking to invert the alpha channel.

The Hue Correct node

The **Hue Correct** node is very useful in that it provides unique control to be able to raise or lower the hue, saturation, and value over the visible color spectrum. The following set of screenshots shows the different effects obtained using similar curves in the **S** and **V** tabs:

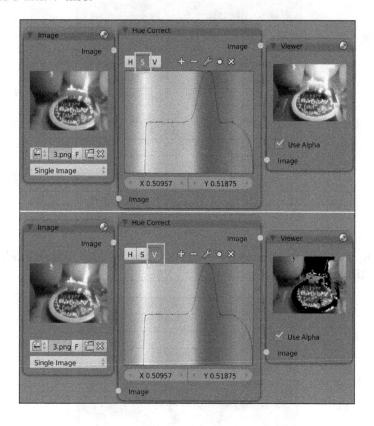

Transformation tools

Transformation tools are used to reposition, reorient, or resize the input footage. Blender is equipped with the **Rotate**, **Translate**, **Scale**, **Flip**, **Crop**, and **Transform** nodes as transformation tools. The following screenshot explains the **Rotate**, **Translate**, and **Scale** nodes:

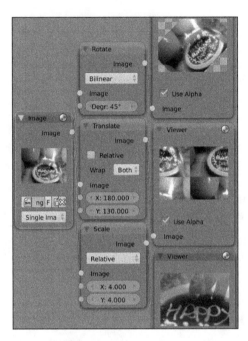

The following screenshot explains the effect of using the **Flip** node's modes **Flip X**, **Flip Y**, and **Flip X & Y**:

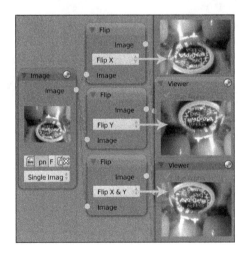

The following screenshot explains how the **Crop** node can be used to modify an image's boundaries:

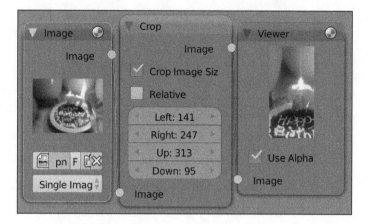

The following screenshot explains how to use the **Transform** node to reposition or reorient an image:

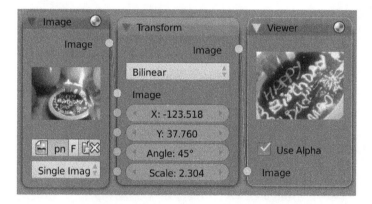

Summary

This chapter explained the multiple techniques that can be used as per your requirements to give a predetermined or desired look to an image.

The next chapter deals with some advanced techniques that are beyond image manipulation in order to make an image look more believable, including various camera effects.

Beyond Grading

5

This chapter deals with advanced compositing beyond grading. These techniques emphasize alternate methods in Blender Compositing for some specific 3D render requirements that can save lots of render time, thereby also saving budgets, in making a CG film. Following is the list of contents that will be presented in this chapter:

- Relighting
- Fresnel effect in compositing
- Depth of Field and Bokeh
- Glares
- Motion and directional blur
- Lens distortions
- Grouping
- UV mapping
- Organizing nodes

Kudos

As the final look of the frame is achieved during the compositing stage, there will always be numerous occasions where there is a requirement for more render passes to finalize the image. This results in extra 3D renders, along with more time and money. Also, few inevitable applications that give life to an image, such as lens effects (Defocus, Glares, and motions blur), are render intensive. Blender Compositor provides alternate procedures for these effects, without having to go back to 3D renders. A well planned CG pipeline can always provide sufficient data to be able to use these techniques during the compositing stage.

Relighting

Relighting is a compositing technique that is used to add extra light information not existing in the received 3D render information. This process facilitates additional creative tweaks in compositing. Though this technique can only provide light without considering shadowing information, additional procedures can provide a convincing approach to this limitation.

The Normal node

Relighting in Blender can be performed using the Normal node. The following screenshot shows the relighting workflow to add a cool light from the right screen. The following illustration uses a **Hue Saturation Value** node to attain the fake light color. Alternatively, any grading nodes can be used for similar effect. The technique is to use the **Dot** output of the **Normal** node as the factor input for any grade node.

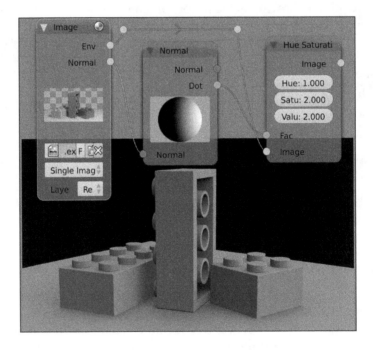

The following screenshot shows relighting with a cyan color light from the top using the Normal node:

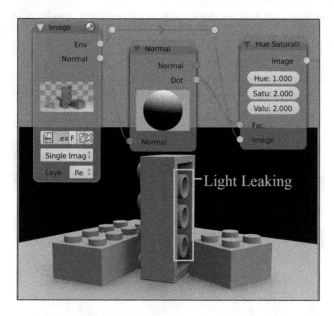

The light direction can be modified by left-clicking and dragging on the diffused sphere thumbnail image provided on the node.

This fake lighting works great when used as secondary light highlights. However, as seen on the vertical brick in the preceding screenshot, light leaks can be encountered as shadowing is not considered. This can often spoil the fun. A quick fix for this is to use the **Ambient Occlusion** information to occlude the unwanted areas.

The following screenshot illustrates the workflow of using the Ambient Occlusion pass along with the normal pass to resolve the light leak issue. The technique is to multiply the dot output of the **Normal** node with Ambient Occlusion info from the rendered image using **Mix** or **Math** nodes. As it can be observed in the following screenshot, the blue light leaks on the inside parts of the vertical brick is minimized by the Ambient Occlusion information. This solution works as long as relighting is not the primary lighting for the scene.

Another issue that can be encountered while using the Normal node is negative values. These values will affect the nonlight areas, leading to an unwanted effect. The procedure to curb these unwanted values is to clamp them from the **Dot** output of the **Normal** node to zero, before using as a mask input to grade nodes.

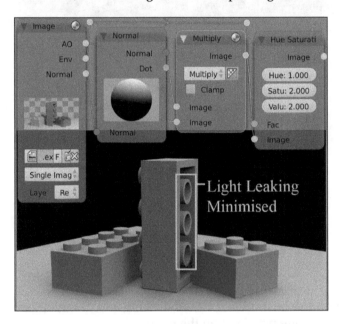

The following screenshot illustrates the issue with negative values. All pixels that have an over-saturated orange color are a result of negative values.

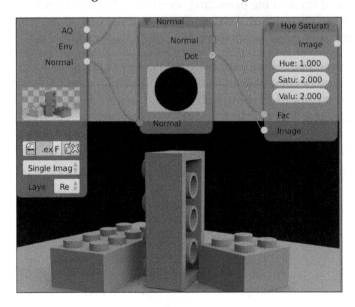

The following screenshot shows the workflow to clamp the negative values from the dot information of a normal pass. A map value is connected between the grade node and **Normal** node, with the **Use Minimum** option on. This makes sure that only negative values are clamped to zero and all other values are unchanged.

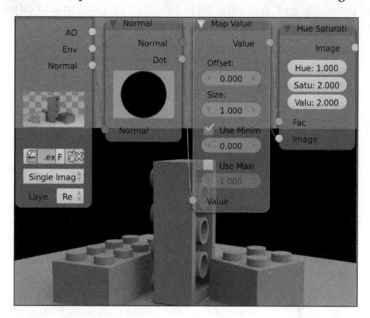

The Fresnel effect

The Fresnel option available in shader parameters is used to modify the reflection intensity, based on the viewing angle, to simulate a metallic behavior. After 3D rendering, altering this property requires rerendering. Blender provides an alternate method to build and modify the Fresnel effect in compositing, using the Normal node.

The following screenshot illustrates the Fresnel workflow. In this procedure, the dot output of a **Normal** node is connected to the **Map Range** node and the **To Min / To Max** values are tweaked to obtain a black-and-white mask map, as shown in the screenshot. A **Math** node is connected to this mask input to clamp information to the 0-1 range.

The 3D-combined render output is rebuilt using the diffuse, specular, and reflection passes from the 3D render. While rebuilding, the mask created using the Normal node should be applied as a mask to the factor input of the reflection **Add** node. This results in applying reflection only to the white areas of the mask, thereby exhibiting the Fresnel effect. A similar technique can be used to add edge highlights, using the mask as a factor input to the grade nodes.

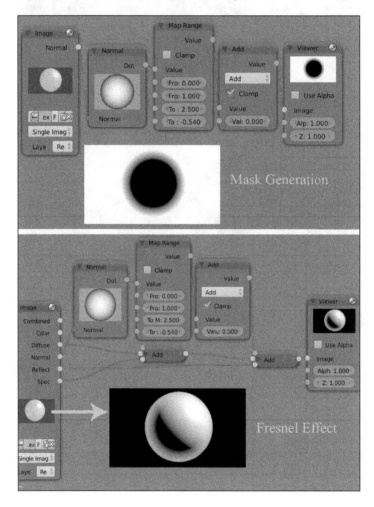

Depth of Field

Depth of Field (DOF) is the simulation of lens focus on the subject of the scene. This effect emphasizes on the subject by blurring everything ahead and behind the subject. In the blurred region, all the tiny highlights expand to exhibit shapes called **Bokeh**.

The Defocus node

Blender provides a Defocus node to simulate DOF. The following screenshot depicts the result of the DOF application as a postprocess in Blender Compositor. From the following screenshot, it can be observed that the emphasis is on the red block, blurring the other blocks and simulating the focus effect. This node requires an image and corresponding Z Depth inputs.

The Bokeh type

The Bokeh type can be set to modify the shape of the Bokeh, emulating a circle, triangle, square, pentagon, hexagon, heptagon, or octagon. Beyond octagon, there will not be any significant difference, as compared to the circle mode. The following screenshot shows different Bokeh shapes on the blue block:

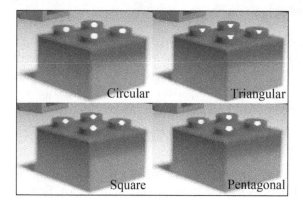

Angle

Angle adds a rotational offset, in degrees, to the chosen Bokeh shape.

Gamma correct

Gamma correct accentuates the Bokeh shape by brightening the out-of-focus areas of the image.

FStop

FStop is a very important parameter that gives control over the focal blur amount. FStop simulates the aperture in a real lens, preserving the luminosity of the image. Similar to a real camera, the smaller the FStop number, the higher the lens iris opening time, and the shallower the Depth of Field. At a default value of 128, everything is in perfect focus, which is assumed as infinity. Half of this value will double the blur amount. This button is available only when enabling **Use Z Buffer**.

Maxblur

Maxblur limits the blur amount of the most out-of-focus regions of the image. Since the Defocus node gets slower to process as the blur amount increases, this value helps limit the maximum blur radius allowed. With a default value of zero, there will not be any limit to the maximum blur amount.

Threshold

When an object that is in-focus overlaps a very far defocused background, aliased edges can be observed. The number of artifacts increases with the increase in distance between the overlapped objects. This value can be used to set how large that blur difference can be, to consider it safe and thereby prevent the occurrence of aliased edges.

Preview

The Preview mode calculates the result a lot faster compared to the Normal mode, using a limited number of (quasi) random samples. This mode also introduces grain, which is the noise in the image (though the noise reduces with more samples). This option should be disabled before rendering.

Use Z-buffer

Enabling the **Use Z-Buffer** option uses the focal point set in the render camera of the 3D Blender scene, as shown in following screenshot. Enabling this option disables Z-Scale.

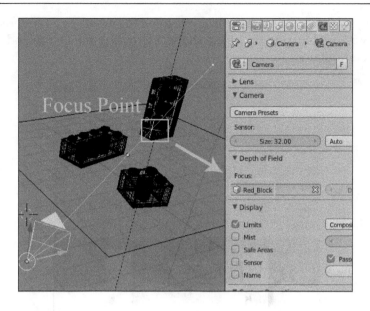

Z-Scale

Using Z-Scale, focus points can me manually adjusted to the required object in the image.

The Bilateral Blur node

The Bilateral Blur node implements a high quality adaptive blur on the source footage. This node can be used to soften a grainy ray-traced Ambient Occlusion pass, smoothing the output from various unbiased renderers. Many heavy performance effects, such as blurry refractions, reflections, and soft shadows can be attained with this node. Its components are as follows:

- **Image**: This is the input image that is to be blurred.
- **Determinator**: This is a source that defines the edges/borders for the blur in the image.
- **Iterations**: This specifies how many times the filter will perform the operation on the image. This actually defines the radius of the blur.
- **Color Sigma**: This specifies the threshold for which the differences of color in the image should be considered as edges.
- **Space Sigma**: This is a fine-tuning variable for the blur radius.

The following screenshot illustrates its application to smoothen a rendered shadow's information without blurring the object shape, by routing the **Depth** and **Normal** data to the determinator:

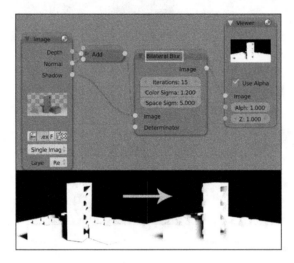

The Blur node

The Blur node can be used as an alternate and fast solution to defocus an image; the effect will not be as appealing as the Defocus node though. Using one of the seven blur modes, this node adds blur to the image, as shown in following screenshot. The radius of the blur is defined by the **X** and **Y** number buttons. Blur is perceived on the image when a value higher than the default zero is used. The **Size** input node can restrict the blur radius as a mask. The values must be mapped between the range of 0-1, as they will be multiplied with the **X** and **Y** number button values.

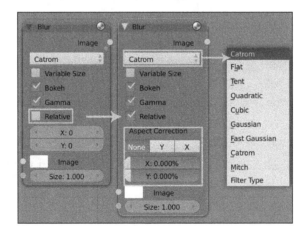

The **X** and **Y** values signify the number of pixels over which the blur effect can spread.

The **Bokeh** button will force the blur node to use a circular blur filter. This node gives a higher quality output, but with higher render times when using the **Bokeh** option. Enabling **Gamma** does gamma correction on the image before blurring it.

Different blur effects can be achieved using different filter types that can be chosen as per the requirement. The following is a list of the types of filter, followed by a screenshot illustrating the blur types:

- **Flat**: This shows everything as uniformly blurred
- **Tent**: This performs a linear falloff by preserving the high and the lows better
- **Quadratic** and **Catrom**: These makes the sharp-contrast edges crisp
- **Cubic** and **Mitch**: These preserve the highs but give an almost out-of-focus blur while softening sharp edges

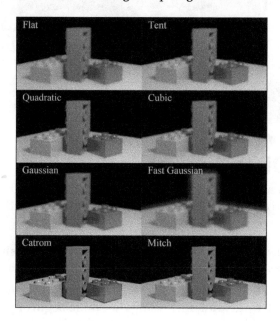

Optical distortions

Every camera lens is bound to have a level of error in it. This leads to luminance drops and patterns such as lens flares, glares, and chromatic aberrations. Some lenses are used to capture images with distorted or enhanced perspectives, such as the fish eye lens and spherical lens. Adding these effects to a CG image will enhance the realism of it. Blender provides a very wide range of nodes to achieve these distortions.

The Glare node

Glare is a discomfort of vision in the presence of a bright source of light. This is seen in any photograph with a light source in its content. This phenomenon exhibits streaks, discs, or foggy rays shooting away from the source. Adding these effects adds realism to the image.

Blender's Glare node provides multiple options to simulate this behavior. The following screenshot illustrates the four types of glares available in Blender's **Glare** node:

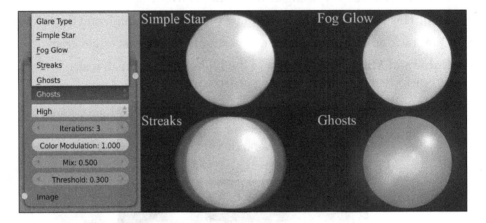

The Lens Distortion node

The Lens Distortion node provides perspective alteration procedures with a chromatic aberration effect, that is, a distortion due to failure of the lens to focus all colors to the same convergence point.

- **Distort**: This can be used to alter the perspective. This value is **0** by default. Increasing this value can lead to perspective distortion.

- **Dispersion**: This can be used to simulate a chromatic aberration effect. This value is **0** by default. Increasing this value begins to show disparity of colors in the edges of the objects/pattern in the image.

- **Jitter**: When enabled, this introduces grain to the image, simulating loss of luminance from lens.

- **Fit**: This can be used to fit the distorted image to a size that covers the empty pixels created due to distortion. Since this resizes the pixels to fit within the resolution, a higher distortion value can show a pixelated image.

All these options can be used in cohesion to obtain multiple lens distortion effects, thus simulating a real world lens and adding more realism to the image.

The following screenshot illustrates the effects that can be obtained using this node. Observe the black/empty pixels created at the bottom corners due to distortion of the perspective.

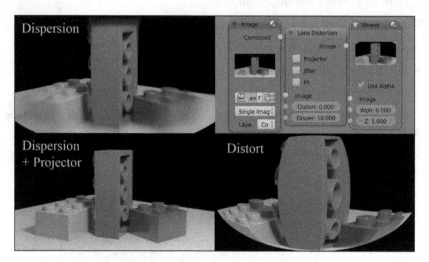

The Despeckle node

The Despeckle node simulates an effect of shattering the pixels. **Threshold** can be used to limit the effect based on the luminance of the image. Alternatively, a gray-scale image can be connected to factor input to control the effect of the Despeckle node, as shown in the following screenshot:

The Filter node

The Filter node implements various image enhancement filters, producing a variety of image distortion effects. The following is a list of filter types available in this node, followed with a screenshot:

- **Soften**: This blurs the image slightly
- **Sharpen**: This increases the contrast, especially at the edges
- **Laplace**: This softens the edges
- **Sobel**: This creates a negative image that highlights the edges
- **Prewitt**: This tries to do what Sobel does, but goes one step better
- **Kirsch**: This is the same as Prewitt or Sobel but gives a better blending on the edges
- **Shadow**: This performs a relief emboss/bump map effect, darkening the outside edges

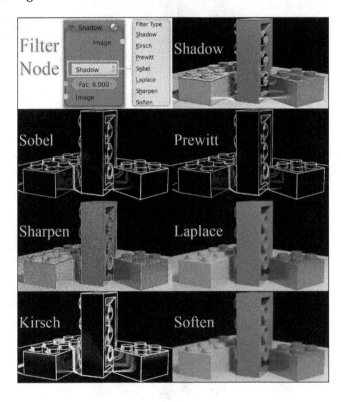

Motion blur

Motion blur is the streaky blur that follows the direction of objects in a motion relative to the camera movement. This is due to long exposure or object/camera rapid motion. Adding this simulation to the composite image also adds realism.

The Vector Blur node

The Vector Blur node in Blender provides an effective motion blur solution in compositing. This node requires vector data and depth data connected to **Speed** and **Z**, respectively.

 Transform information of a specific point travelled in relation to the previous and next frames is stored as a vector pass, also called **Motion Vectors**.

The following is list of the Vector Blur node attributes:

- **Samples**: This defines the quality of the blur
- **Blur**: This specifies the amount of the blur in pixels
- **Min**: This is the threshold for the slowest moving points of the image
- **Max**: This is the threshold for the fastest moving points of the image

The following screenshot illustrates **Motion Blur**, simulated using the **Vector Blur** node:

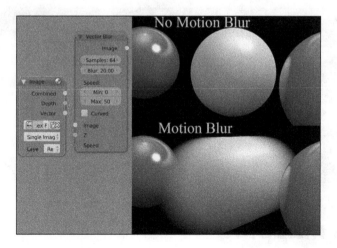

The Directional Blur node

The Directional Blur node can be used to create a fake motion blur effect by blurring an image in a specified direction and magnitude. This can be used as a faster solution for Vector Blur, in specific cases. Since this is a fake blur, it blurs all points on the image, without considering the movement of the points. Its parameters are as follows:

- **Iterations**: This controls the number of times the image is duplicated to create the blur effect. Higher values give smoother results.
- **Wrap**: This wraps the image on the x and y axis to fill in areas that become transparent from the blur effect.
- **Center**: This sets the position for the blur center. It makes a difference if Angle, Spin, and/or Zoom options are used.
- **Distance**: This regulates the largeness of the blur effect.
- **Angle**: This blurs the image at the angle specified from the center.
- **Spin**: This rotates the image at each iteration to create a spin effect from the center point.
- **Zoom**: This scales the image at each iteration, creating the effect of a zoom.

The following screenshot illustrates the utilization of the Directional Blur node. It can be observed that all the spheres are now blurred in a specified direction, unlike in Vector Blur, where only the center sphere was in motion. In many rapid motion scenes in which the scene subjects are far from the camera, this effect can give a believable and faster result.

Texture mapping

Texture mapping in compositing is yet another time-saving technique that facilitates in wrapping a texture to a mesh. The UV pass, as a 32-bit float image, is required to perform this wrapping.

The Map UV node

The Map UV node in Blender should be used to perform texture mapping at the compositing stage.

As illustrated in the following screenshot, a **Texture** and **UV Pass** have to be connected to the respective sockets of the **Map UV** node to attain the wrapping. As seen in the following example, the sphere and plane rendered without any textures are wrapped with a texture using a map UV node.

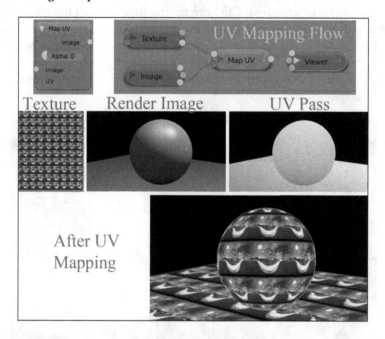

This technique allows the user to be able to modify specific object textures in compositing without needing a 3D rerendering. This can save a huge amount of time in the CG film production process, where creative changes are bound to happen at any stage.

Organizing

Organizing plays a major role in CG production. It can increase efficiency by gaining consistency. Organizing the master flows (flows done for a few typical shots that will be replicated on similar shots after getting the director's approval) will make it easy to replicate or reuse them for other shots. This also reduces confusion when relooking at the flow over a period of time. Blender provides the following methods to organize the flow.

Grouping

Grouping is a method of gathering a node network and converting it to one node. This group can be reused any number of times with the same functionality. This also makes the flow less cumbersome.

- *Ctrl + G* is the shortcut key for grouping a selected node network
- *Alt + G* is the shortcut key for ungrouping

In the following screenshot, the relighting network built to create a fake top blue light can be selected and grouped. Clicking on the link icon on the top right of the group node will open the network inside the group with a pale green backdrop. Clicking on the Go to parent node tree icon, as shown in following screenshot, will switch back to the actual node network. Alternatively, the *Tab* key can be used to switch in and out of group levels. Multiple levels of groupings can be made to form nested groups.

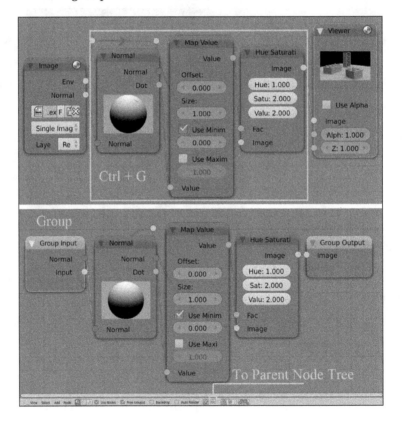

The group can be renamed by selecting the group node; press *N* to open the **Properties** window and modify the name under node name, as shown in following screenshot. All groups of the current file can be found by navigating to the **Add | Group** menu.

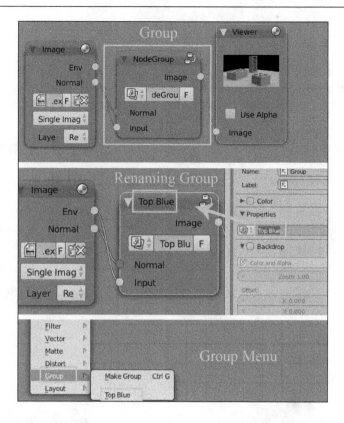

The input and output sockets can be renamed in the properties panel, accessed by the *N* key, as shown in the following screenshot:

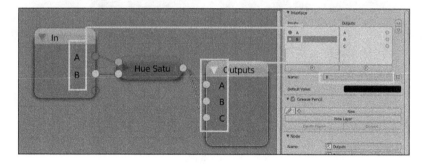

Layout

The **Layout** options in Blender Compositor allow the user to discriminate and define parts of the flow, thus increasing the readability and understanding of the flow significance. The **Add | Layout** menu item displays the layout options available in Blender.

Frame

As shown in the following screenshot, **Frame** can be added as a backdrop to a group of nodes to add a note, specifying the significance of the network. Each frame can be given a specific color to emphasize the significance. Notes can be added in the **Label** textbox under the **Properties** panel of the frame. Similarly, the frame color can be modified in the **Color Presets** textbox.

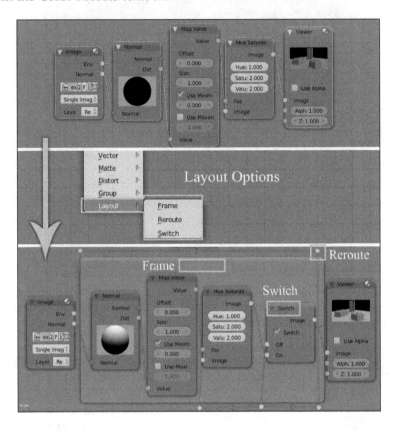

Reroute

Often, the nodes will overlap the noodle connections or overlapping connections, making things confusing. Using Reroute, the connections can be organized. Left-clicking on a noodle with the *Shift* key pressed on the keyboard will also add the Reroute node.

Switch

Switch can be used in specific cases where a portion of the network needs to be bypassed, but doesn't need to be deleted from the flow.

Summary

This chapter dealt with several advanced techniques, such as Motion blur, Defocus, optical distortions, and UV mapping, that can save project time. This chapter also described efficient ways of organizing the flow for reuse or sharing, boosting efficiency to hit the targets.

The next chapter will illustrate masking, keying, and filtering techniques.

6
Alpha Sports

This chapter starts by providing an understanding of the significance of an alpha channel and some issues related to it. After realizing the alpha channel, this chapter deals with different keying and masking techniques. Following is the list of topics covered in this chapter:

- Significance of the alpha channel
- Blender's alpha modes
- Layering concept and formula
- Using the alpha channel when layering the foreground over the background with the Mix and Alpha Over nodes
- Solving fringing issues while using the alpha channel with the Mix and Alpha Over nodes
- Generating matte masks using the ID Mask node
- Different ways to invert matte information
- Edge filtering
- Value and luminance
- Concept of keying and what to inspect in the footage to be keyed
- Understanding Blender's keying nodes

What is an Alpha channel?

The alpha channel first introduced by *Alvy Ray Smith* in the 1970s, can store values between 0-1, signifying whether a specific pixel is transparent, opaque, or semitransparent. Though this channel is boring to look at, this information is very essential when merging footages. Alpha information can be stored either independent of RGB, referred to as **straight alpha**, or by multiplying it with RGB, referred to as **premultiplied alpha**. A value of zero in the alpha channels signifies that the RGB pixel should be completely transparent, and opaque when the value is one. The following screenshot portrays an alpha channel:

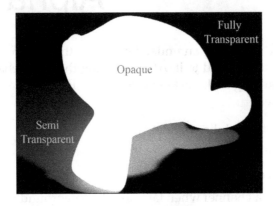

Alpha modes in Blender

As shown in the following screenshot, Blender has two alpha modes. The **Transparent** mode considers transparency parameters in shaders and accordingly generates the pixel value for alpha. The **Sky** mode considers sky as opaque, thereby making the alpha channel completely white.

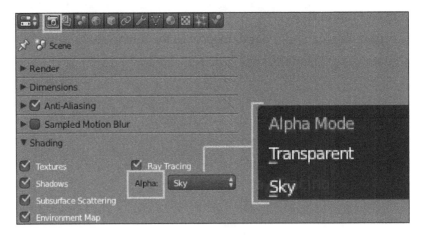

The following screenshot represents alpha, rendered with the **Sky Mode**:

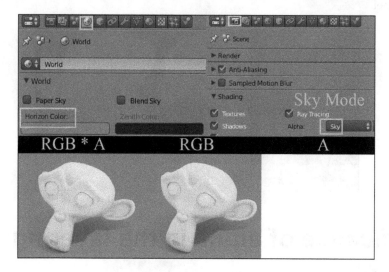

The following screenshot represents alpha, rendered with the **Transparency** mode:

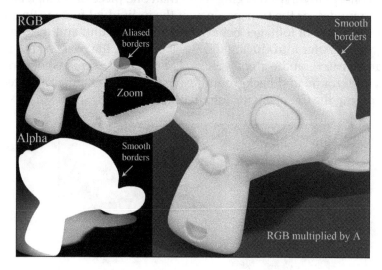

Visualizing alpha in Blender

Blender provides three different drawing modes to view alpha with respect to the image RGB channel. As shown in the following screenshot, these options can be seen in the menu panel of the UV/Image Editor. The **RGB * A** mode displays RGB with premultiplied alpha, the **RGB** mode displays only RGB information, and the **A** mode displays only alpha channel information in the image.

The **RGB** mode draws the RGB channel with "aliased" edges, since it doesn't consider the alpha channel.

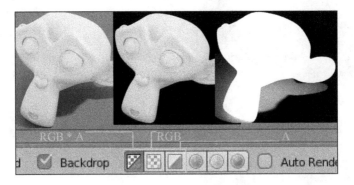

Significance of alpha in the layering concept

The layering concept involves merging more than one piece of footage based on the color, blending modes, or the transparency of the individual footage. In either of the cases, one of the pieces of footages behaves as the foreground and the other behaves as the background. After introducing the alpha channel, the background information perceived can be based on the alpha values. The following screenshot shows the layering of a foreground and background using the alpha channel. This technique is vital for merging the CG elements into live shot footage.

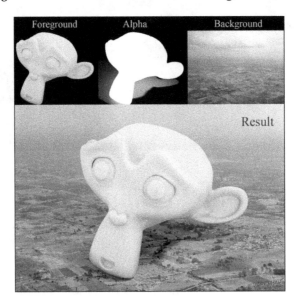

Following is the layering formula used in the type of layering we just discussed:

 (FG * A) + (BG(1- A)) = Result, where FG stands for the foreground image, BG stands for the background image, and A stands for FG Alpha.

Layering in Blender with the alpha channel

To perform layering in Blender Compositing, the alpha channel can be used either with the Mix node or Alpha Over node.

Layering with the Mix node

The following screenshot depicts the process of layering using a Mix node. A background image is connected to the upper **Image** socket and a foreground image to the lower **Image** socket of the Mix node. Now the result shows only the aliased RGB channel of the foreground. If the foreground image has an alpha channel associated, then **Include Alpha Toggle** should be used in the **Mix** node, as shown in following screenshot:

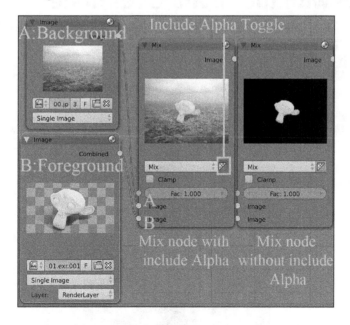

If the foreground image doesn't have the alpha channel, then a separate alpha image can be fed to the **Fac** socket of the Mix node to obtain the same result. Alternatively, if the combined channel is accessible, then a **Separate RGBA** converter node can be used to extract the alpha channel from the combined pass information and can be fed to the **Fac** input of the Mix node, as shown in the following screenshot:

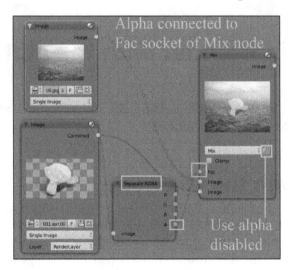

Layering with the Alpha Over node

Layering using the Alpha Over node can be performed by connecting a background image to the upper **Image** socket and a foreground image to the lower **Image** socket of the Alpha Over node, as shown in the following screenshot:

Fringe issue

When the resulting images from the Alpha Over and Mix layering techniques are compared, a one-pixel dark line can be seen on the edge of the foreground content in the Mix layering mode, but not seen in Alpha Over process. This is termed as **Fringe issue**, as shown in the following screenshot:

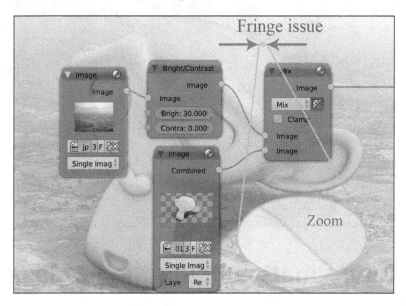

At first, it might seem that the Mix node is messy, but this difference is due to the way both the nodes assume whether the alpha input is premultiplied or straight. When using the transparent alpha mode, Blender renders the image with a premultiplied alpha. Since the Alpha Over node assumes that the input is premultiplied by default, it performs calculations correctly. However, the Mix node assumes that the input has a straight alpha.

To solve the issue, an Alpha Convert node should be connected to the lower **Image** socket of the **Mix** node. By selecting the **Premul to Straight** mode in the Alpha Convert node, the straight alpha mode is created from premultiplied alpha input. When this is fed to the Mix node, this fringe issue is resolved.

The following screenshot represents the use of the Alpha Convert node to solve the fringe issue for a Mix node, with the transparent alpha mode being used:

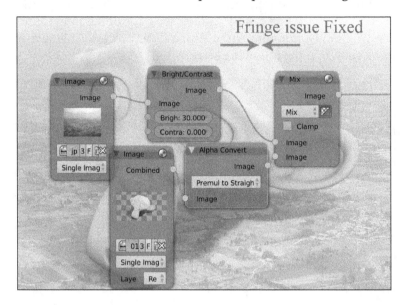

Generating mattes using the ID Mask node

There will be many instances during CG compositing where a few specific meshes in the image would require a mask pass. This provides control to modify specific pixels. To obtain these mattes, the ID Mask node can be used along with the information stored in **Object Index** or **Material Index** passes.

When given a value for the index, the ID Mask node creates a mask for the meshes that have the same value assigned as their **Pass Index** value, as shown in the following screenshot. All these **Pass Index** values of meshes can be obtained using the Object Index pass. The Object or Material Index pass has to be connected to the **ID value** socket of the **ID Mask** node, for the node to pick the **Index** values. The generated mask information can be used as an input for the **Fac** sockets available to many Blender nodes to affect only the required mesh.

In the following screenshot, assigning **Pass Index** to one of the three cubes and enabling the **Object Index** pass is explained. When the Object Index pass from this example is plugged into the **ID value** socket of the **ID Mask** node and a value of **2** is given as the index value to the **ID Mask** node, it outputs the mask of the blue cube.

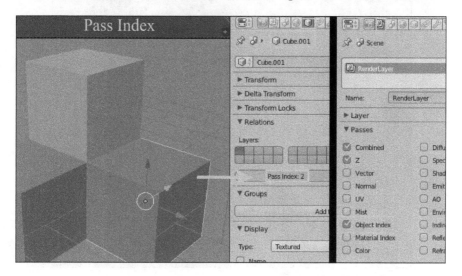

The following screenshot shows how the blue cube mask is created using the **ID Mask** node, using the Object Index pass:

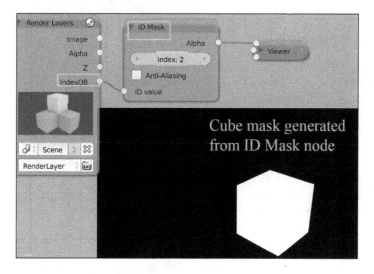

Now that the mask for the blue cube is available, this blue cube can be converted to a pale and bright colored cube, with the flow explained in following screenshot:

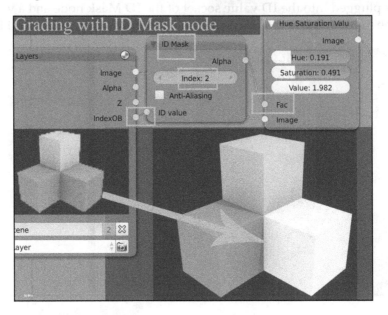

Similar to Object Index, Material Index can also be used with the ID Mask node. Material Index is available in the **Material** option.

Edge filtering

Sometimes, the edges of the alpha need to be expanded or blurred to obtain a specific effect or to soften the aliased edges. This effect can be achieved using the Blur and ColorRamp nodes in cohesion.

To blur the mask generated for the blue cube, it has to be connected to a Blur node and the Blur node has to be connected to the ColorRamp node, as shown in the following screenshot. Now, by increasing the **X** and **Y** values in the **Blur** node, the mask area can be expanded or contracted. Using the black and white handles in the **ColorRamp** node, the edge of the modified mask can be softened or sharpened. This process of altering the mask boundary is termed as **edge filtering**.

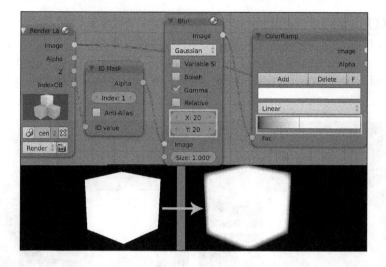

Inverting values

Sometimes, it's faster to invert a mask or RGB tones rather than recreating a new one. Though there is an **Invert** node to do this, it's worth understanding how the same effect can be obtained using a different node. This can enhance the perception on node utilizations, as shown in the following screenshot:

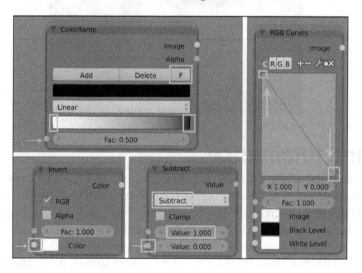

The previous screenshot explains multiple ways to invert an image. Using the *F* key on the ColorRamp node to invert the black and white handles, subtracting the input from 1 using a Math node, and reversing the default curve in RGB curves node will result in inverting the input image.

Keying

Keying, also known as **chroma keying** or **color keying**, is the process of converting a specific range of colors into the alpha channel, to show the background footage when layered. The following screenshot shows an example of this concept:

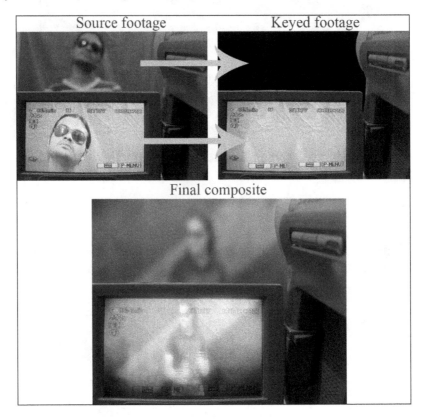

Value and luminance

A clear understanding of the differences between value and luminance is very essential in compositing since the human eye is more sensitive to luminance than to colors. It turns out to be even more crucial while keying, since everything in keying is dependent on how you start the process, with respect to a specific channel in a specific color space. To explain this in detail, the following screenshot will be used, which contains different tones with at least one of the RGB components having a value of **1**:

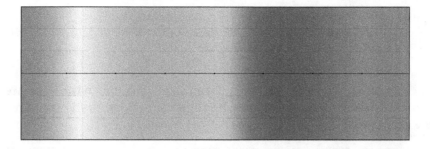

The **desaturation** of an image will result in displaying the value of the image. The value displays the maximum value in between the RGB components. Since the input image has the value as **1** in any one of the RGB channels, the result will be a full white image signifying a value of 1 in any of the colors, existing as the maximum value in any of the channels.

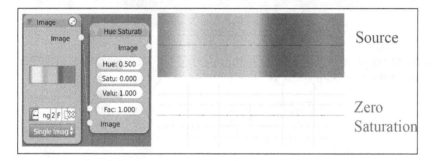

Luminance

When we see the colors, we can perceive perceive blue as dark color compared to Cyan and Yellow as bright compared to red. This variation in brightness that we perceive is called the **luminance** of the color.

Luminance of an image can be displayed using the **RGB to BW** node. The following screenshot illustrates the luminance levels of colors when using the RGB to BW node:

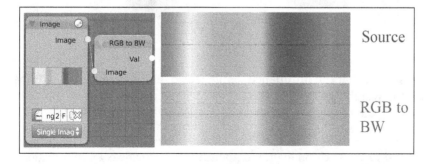

[It has to be understood that the desaturation of an image is not the same as making it into a black-and-white image.]

Luminance of the same image, when displayed as a **Y** channel in the **Separate YUVA** node, also shows the variation of brightness in colors, as shown in the following screenshot:

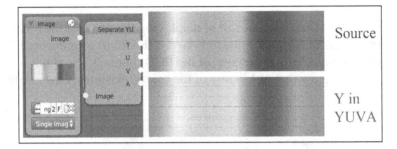

The following screenshot shows the luminance of the same image using three different modes of the **Separate YCbCrA** node:

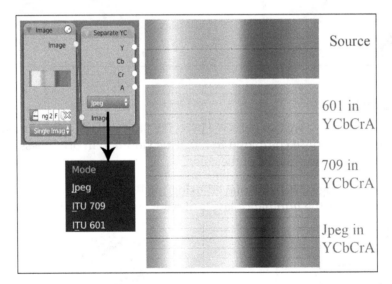

It can be observed that the luminance displayed in all these models is not the same since the weightage of 100 percent for each channel in RGB is different in each model. So, the model to be chosen depends on the requirement.

- **Y** in YUVA is the same as **Y** in YCbCrA in the **Jpeg** mode
- UV and CbCr are chrominance components that provide color information

After having a good understanding of luminance and the different models available, an apt model can be chosen as a starting point in keying, where the color ranges to be keyed are close to blacks or whites in a specific color model.

Inspecting a green/blue screen footage

The success of keying green/blue screen footage depends on the following factors. These have to be inspected before proceeding to keying.

- The color to be keyed should have consistent lighting
- The subjects should be far enough from the green/blue screen, to avoid color spill
- The subjects should be lit properly
- The footage should be uncompressed

The Difference Key node

The Difference Key node creates a mask based on the difference between the inputs plugged to the **Image 1** and **Image 2** sockets. **Tolerance** and **Falloff** can be adjusted to fine-tune the created mask. The following screenshot shows an example using the **Difference Key** node to modify the flower tone:

The Distance Key node

The **Distance Key** node works similar to the Difference Key node but with a different algorithm. **Tolerance** and **Falloff** can be adjusted to fine-tune the created mask.

The Luminance Key node

The Luminance Key node creates a mask based on luminance of the input plugged to the **Image** socket, controlled by **Low** and **High** handles. This node works as per the YUVA color space. The following screenshot shows an example using the **Luminance Key** node to modify the flower tone:

The Color Key node

The Color Key node creates a mask based on the sampled color in the key color area. HSV sliders can be adjusted to the generated mask.

The Channel Key node

The Channel Key node provides options to select any component in any color space to start creating a mask. **High** and **Low** sliders can be used to modify the generated mask as per the requirements. The following screenshot shows an example using **Key Channel** to modify the flower tone:

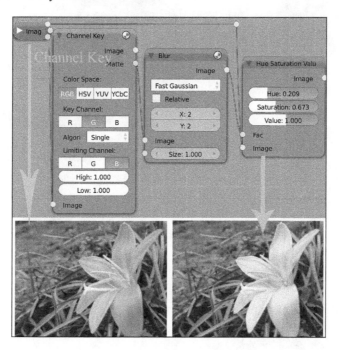

Summary

This chapter explained the significance of the alpha channel and how to create or manipulate alpha masks using Object Index and keying techniques. A very important understanding about the difference between value and luminance was also covered in this chapter.

Using all the different concepts and techniques explained in this book, many complex Blender node trees related to VFX or CG animation can be created. Based on the desired effect, a specific technique or a group of techniques explained in this book can be applied.

Index

Hue slider, Hue Saturation Value node 35

I

ID Mask node
  used, for generating mattes 80-82
image color depth 8
image input/output system 8
image manipulation
  about 34
  Bright/Contrast node 34
  Color Balance node 42
  Color Correction node 36
  gamma node 46
  Hue Correct node 47
  Hue Saturation Value node 35
  Invert node 47
  Mix node 43
  RGB Curves node 39
  transformation tools 48
Image node 27
Include Alpha Toggle 77
input nodes 16
  about 25
  Bokeh Image node 29
  Image node 27
  Mask node 28
  Movie Clip node 27
  Render Layers node 26
  RGB node 27
  Texture node 28
  Time node 28
  Value Node 27
Invert node 47

K

keying
  about 84
  Channel Key node 89
  Color Key node 88
  Difference Key node 87
  Distance Key node 88
  green/blue screen footage, inspecting 87
  luminance 84-86

Luminance Key node 88
value desaturation 85

L

layering
  Fringe issue 79
  performing, with alpha channel 77
  performing, with Alpha Over node 78
layering concept
  about 76
  alpha channel, used 76
layout options
  about 69
  frame 70
  reroute 71
  switch 71
Lens Distortion node 62
Levels node 31
Lift property, Color Correction node 39
linear workspace 23
luminance 85
Luminance Key node 88

M

Map UV node 67
Mask node 28
Mask socket, Color Correction node 39
mattes
  generating, ID Mask node used 80-82
Maxblur 58
Mix node
  about 43
  blending modes 44
  Fac socket 78
  factor input field 45
  Use Alpha button 45
  used, for layering 77
motion blur
  about 65
  Directional Blur node 66
  Vector Blur node 65
Motion Vectors 65
Movie Clip node 27

transformation nodes 16
transformation tools 48, 49
transparent mode, alpha 74

U

UI, Blenders Compositor
  node editor 18, 19
  UV Image Editor 16, 20
Use Alpha button, Mix node 45
UV Image Editor 16, 20, 21
UV Pass 67

V

value desaturation 85
Value node 27

values
  inverting 83
Vector Blur node, motion blur 65
Viewer node 30

Y

YCbCr color space 10
YUV color space 9

Z

Z-buffer
  enabling 58
Z-Scale
  using 59

Thank you for buying
Blender Compositing and Post Processing

About Packt Publishing

Packt, pronounced 'packed', published its first book "*Mastering phpMyAdmin for Effective MySQL Management*" in April 2004 and subsequently continued to specialize in publishing highly focused books on specific technologies and solutions.

Our books and publications share the experiences of your fellow IT professionals in adapting and customizing today's systems, applications, and frameworks. Our solution based books give you the knowledge and power to customize the software and technologies you're using to get the job done. Packt books are more specific and less general than the IT books you have seen in the past. Our unique business model allows us to bring you more focused information, giving you more of what you need to know, and less of what you don't.

Packt is a modern, yet unique publishing company, which focuses on producing quality, cutting-edge books for communities of developers, administrators, and newbies alike. For more information, please visit our website: www.packtpub.com.

About Packt Open Source

In 2010, Packt launched two new brands, Packt Open Source and Packt Enterprise, in order to continue its focus on specialization. This book is part of the Packt Open Source brand, home to books published on software built around Open Source licences, and offering information to anybody from advanced developers to budding web designers. The Open Source brand also runs Packt's Open Source Royalty Scheme, by which Packt gives a royalty to each Open Source project about whose software a book is sold.

Writing for Packt

We welcome all inquiries from people who are interested in authoring. Book proposals should be sent to author@packtpub.com. If your book idea is still at an early stage and you would like to discuss it first before writing a formal book proposal, contact us; one of our commissioning editors will get in touch with you.

We're not just looking for published authors; if you have strong technical skills but no writing experience, our experienced editors can help you develop a writing career, or simply get some additional reward for your expertise.

Blender 2.6 Cycles: Materials and Textures Cookbook

ISBN: 978-1-78216-130-1   Paperback: 280 pages

Over 40 recipes to help you create stunning materials and textures using the Cycles rendering engine with Blender

1. Create naturalistic materials and textures - such as rock, snow, ice and fire - using Cycles

2. Learn Cycle's node-based material system

3. Get to grips with the powerful Cycles rendering engine

Blender 3D Basics

ISBN: 978-1-84951-690-7   Paperback: 468 pages

The complete novice's guide to 3D modeling and animation

1. The best starter guide for complete newcomers to 3D modeling and animation

2. Easier learning curve than any other book on Blender

3. You will learn all the important foundation skills ready to apply to any 3D software

Please check **www.PacktPub.com** for information on our titles

Blender Game Engine Beginner's Guide

ISBN: 978-1-84951-702-7   Paperback: 206 pages

The non programmer's guide to creating 3D video games

1. Use Blender to create a complete 3D video game

2. Ideal entry level to game development without the need for coding

3. No programming or scripting required

Blender 2.5 Character Animation Cookbook

ISBN: 978-1-84951-320-3   Paperback: 308 pages

50 great recipes for giving soul to your characters by building high-quality rigs and understanding the principles of movement

1. Learn how to create efficient and easy-to-use character rigs

2. Understand and make your characters , so that your audience believes they're alive

3. See common approaches when animating your characters in real world situations

Please check **www.PacktPub.com** for information on our titles

www.ingramcontent.com/pod-product-compliance
Lightning Source LLC
Chambersburg PA
CBHW060158060326
40690CB00018B/4161